FIRST 50
CLASSICAL PIECES
YOU SHOULD PLAY ON GUITAR

Compiled and Edited by John Hill

ISBN 978-1-4950-5657-4

HAL•LEONARD®
CORPORATION
7777 W. BLUEMOUND RD. P.O. BOX 13819 MILWAUKEE, WI 53213

In Australia Contact:
Hal Leonard Australia Pty. Ltd.
4 Lentara Court
Cheltenham, Victoria, 3192 Australia
Email: ausadmin@halleonard.com.au

Visit Hal Leonard Online at
www.halleonard.com

CONTENTS

Adelita
(Mazurka)

Francisco Tárrega
(1852 - 1909)

Lento

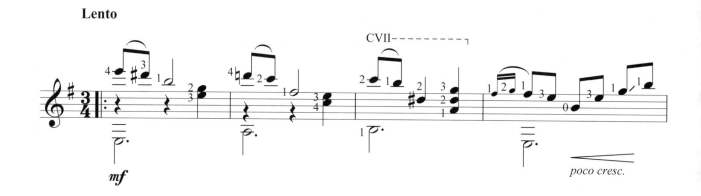

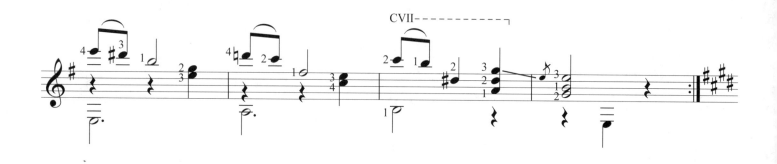

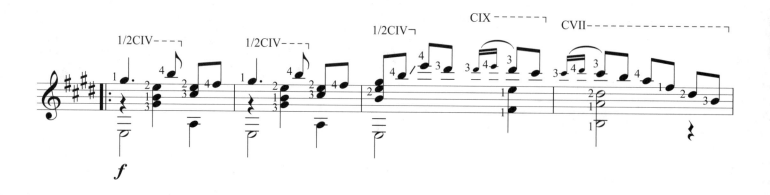

Aria

David Kellner
(1670 - 1748)

Allegro
BWV 998

Johann Sebastian Bach
(1685-1750)

Tuning:
(low to high) D-A-D-G-B-E

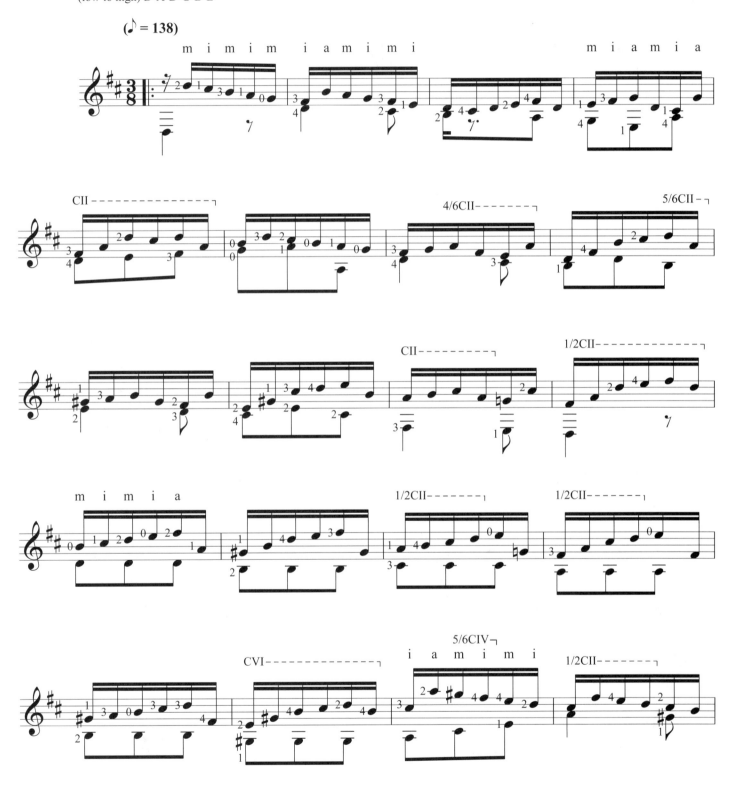

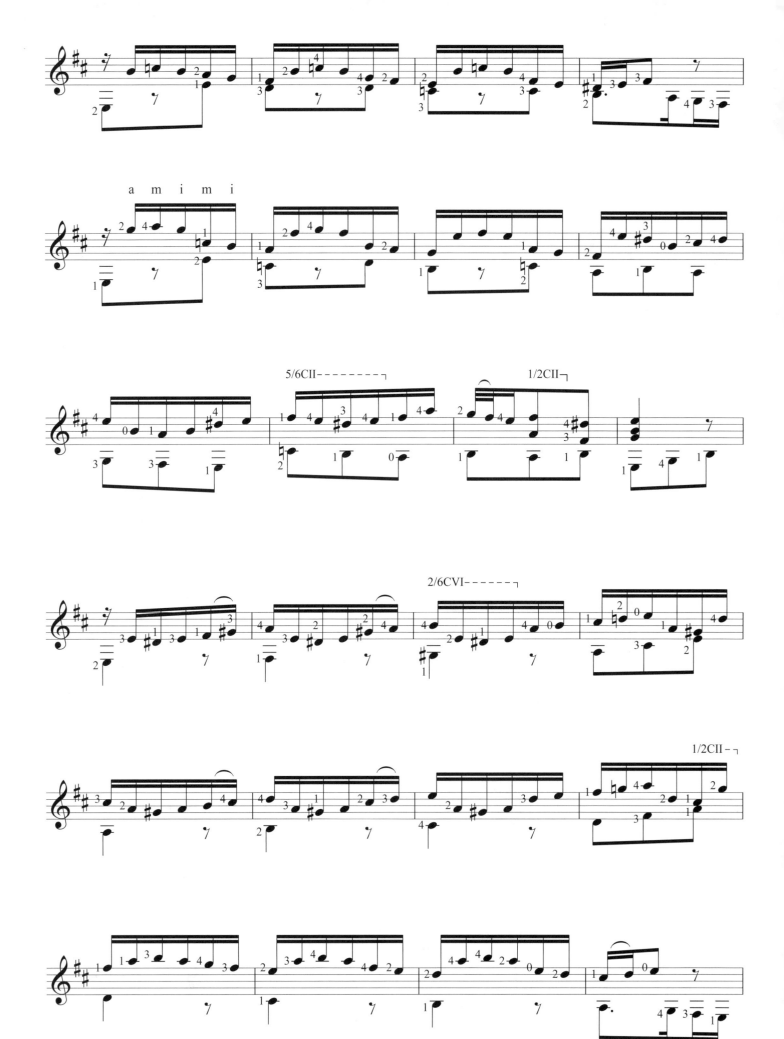

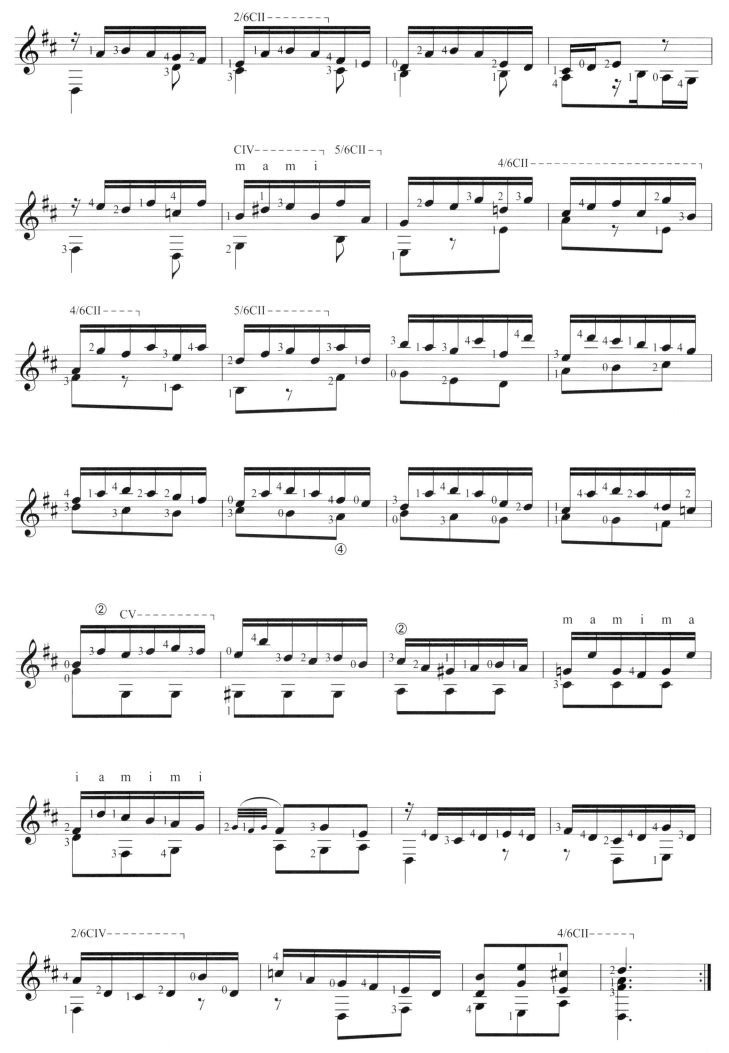

Allegro

from CONCERTO FOR LUTE AND STRINGS IN D MAJOR, RV 93

Antonio Vivaldi
(1678 - 1741)

Largo

from CONCERTO FOR LUTE AND STRINGS IN D MAJOR, RV 93

Antonio Vivaldi
(1678 - 1741)

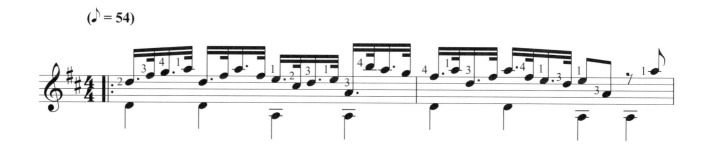

Allegro

from CONCERTO FOR LUTE AND STRINGS IN D MAJOR, RV 93

Antonio Vivaldi
(1678 - 1741)

Allemande

from LUTE SUITE NO. 1, BWV 996

Johann Sebastian Bach
(1685-1750)

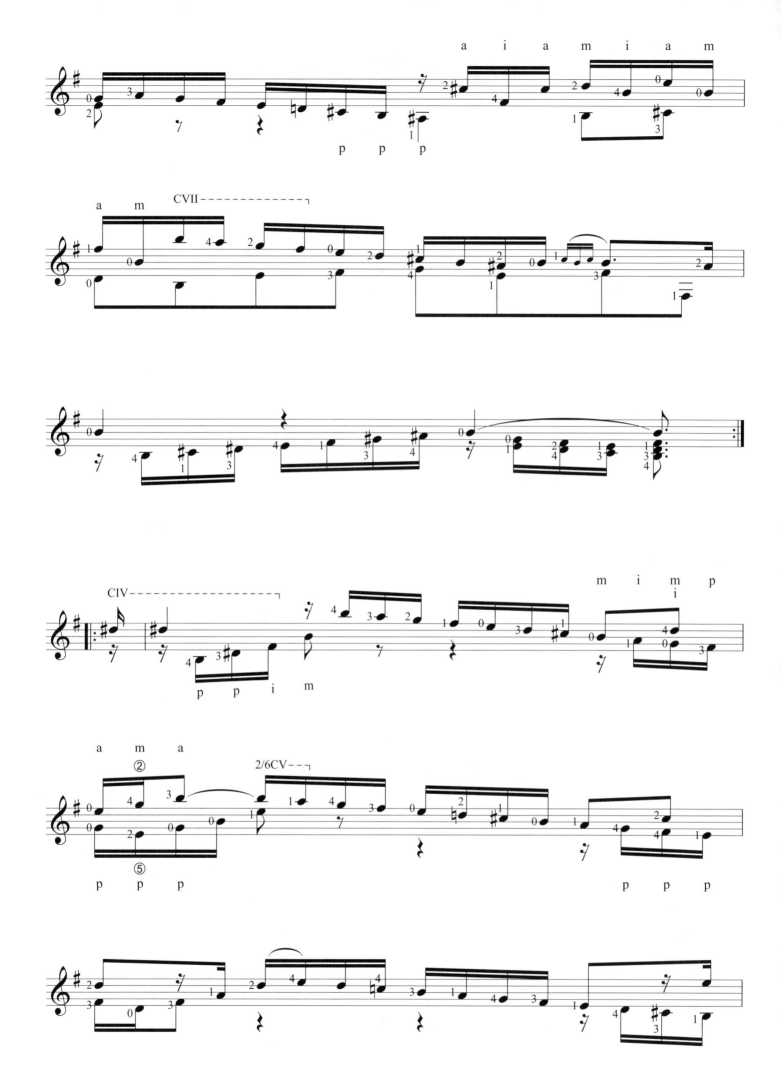

Andante Religioso

from LA CATEDRAL*

Augustín Barrios
(1886 - 1944)

Moderato

*Prelude "Saudade" is not included in this collection due to copyright restriction.

23

Allegro Solemne

from LA CATEDRAL*

Augustín Barrios
(1886 - 1944)

*Prelude "Saudade" is not included in this collection due to copyright restriction.

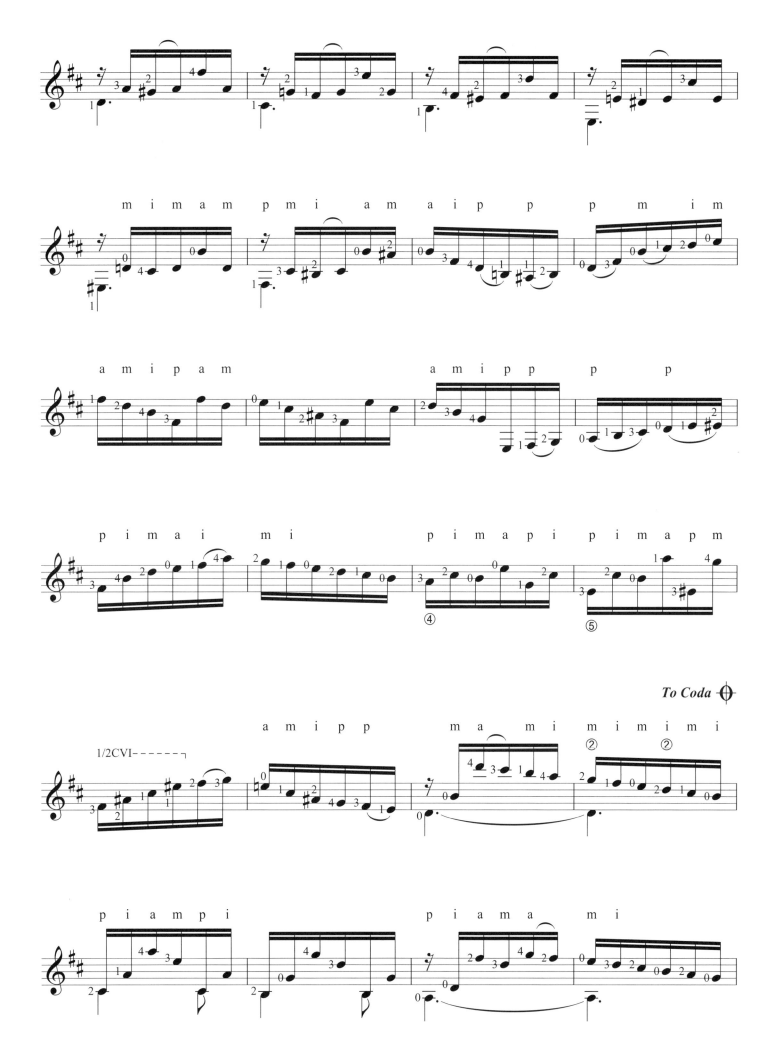

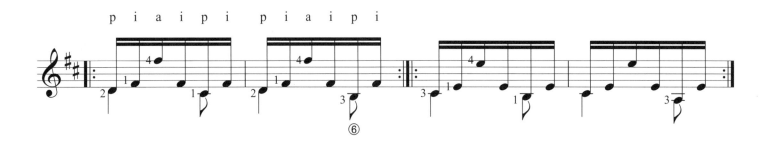

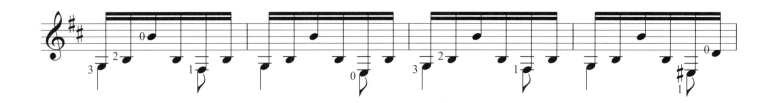

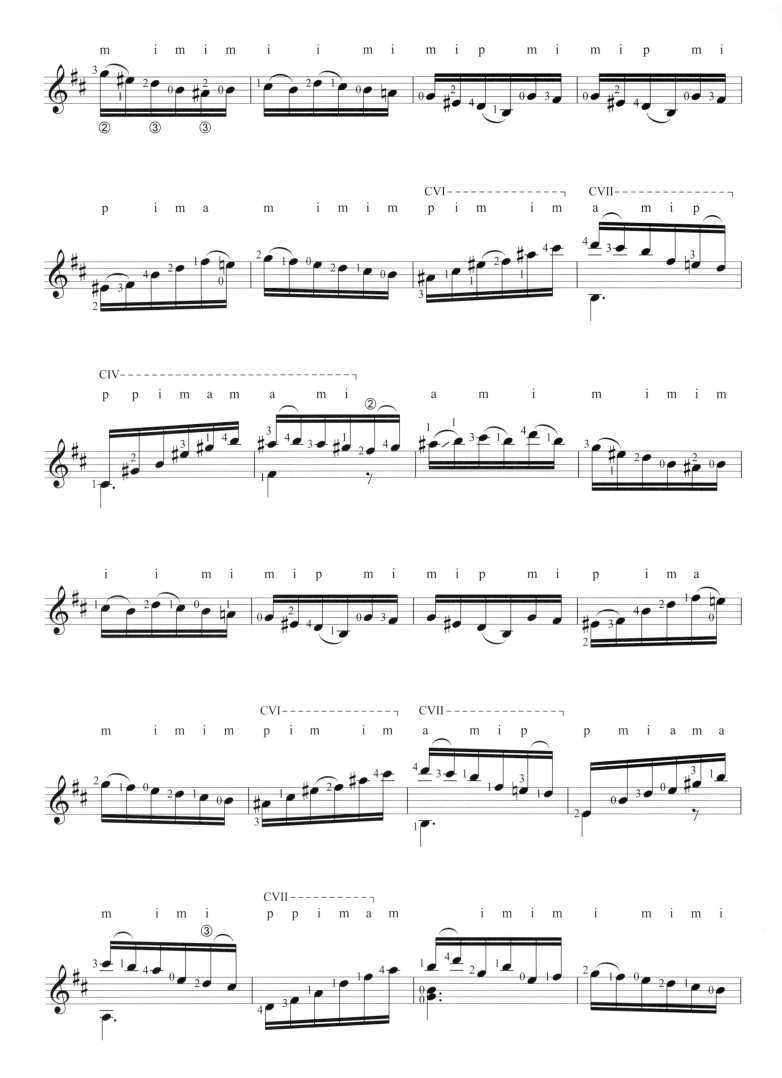

D.S. al Coda

Coda

Bianco Fiore

Anonymous
(c. 1600)

Tuning:
(low to high) D-A-D-G-B-E

Bourée

Robert de Visée
(c. 1650 - 1720)

Bourrée

from LUTE SUITE NO. 1, BWV 996

Johann Sebastian Bach
(1685 - 1750)

Canarios

Gaspar Sanz
(1640 - 1710)

Tuning:
(low to high) D-A-D-G-B-E

Diferencias sobre "Guárdame las vacas"

from LOS SEYS LIBROS DEL DELPHIN DE MUSICA, 1538

Luis de Narváez
(c. 1490 - 1547)

El Noi de la Mare
(The Son of Mary)

Miguel Llobet
(1878 - 1922)

Tuning:
(low to high) D-A-D-G-B-E

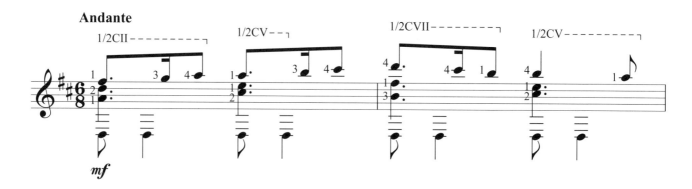

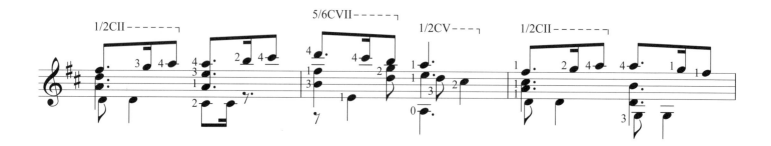

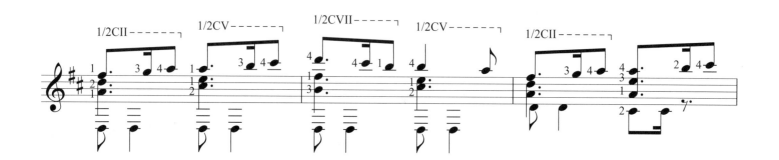

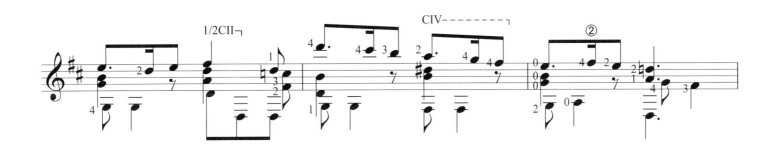

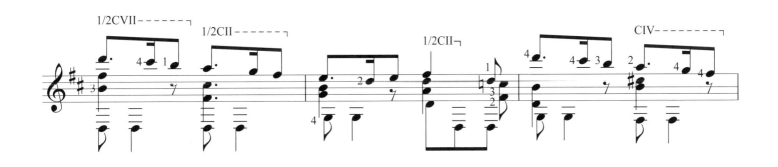

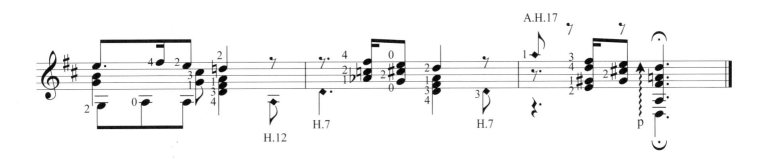

El Testament d'Amelia

Catalan Folk Song

Tuning:
(low to high) D-A-D-G-B-E

Andante

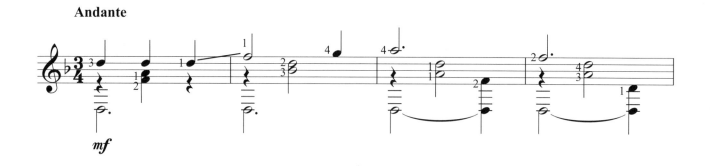

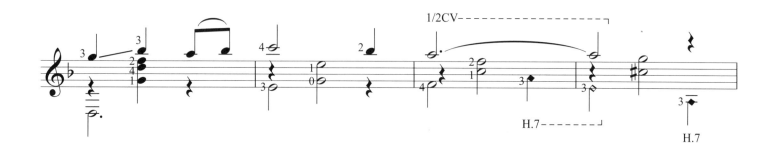

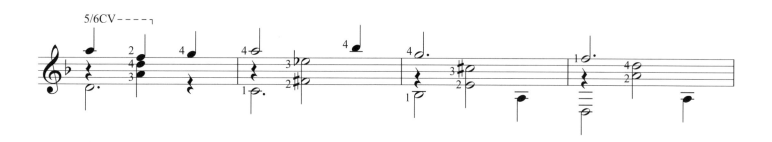

40

D.C. al Coda

Coda

Fantasie

Silvius Leopold Weiss
(1686 - 1750)

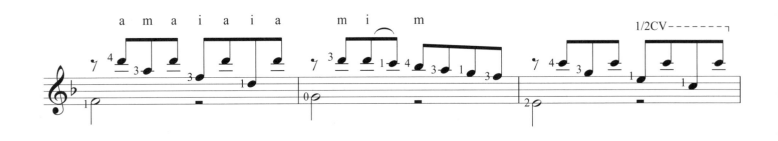

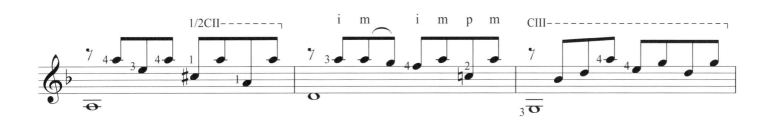

Gagliarda

Anonymous
(c. 1600)

Tuning:
(low to high) D-A-D-G-B-E

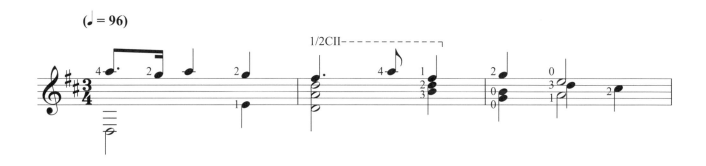

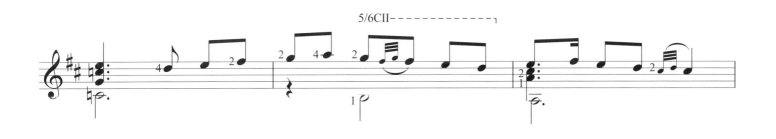

Gavotte

Robert de Visée
(c. 1650 - 1720)

Gavotte

Lodovico Roncalli
(1654 - 1713)

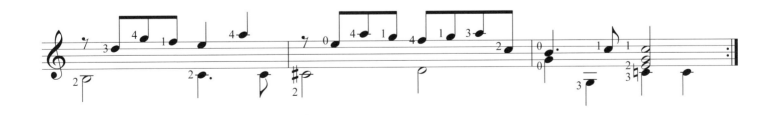

Gigue

from LUTE SUITE NO. 1, BWV 996

Johann Sebastian Bach
(1685 - 1750)

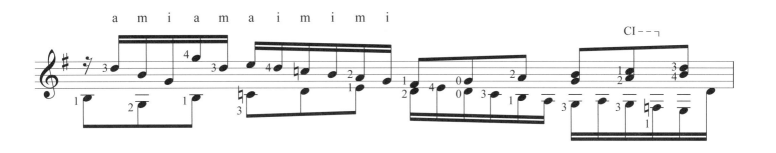

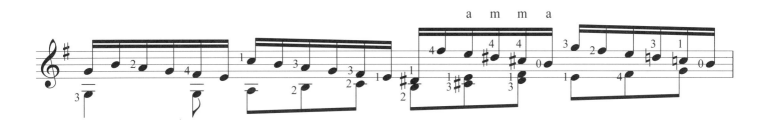

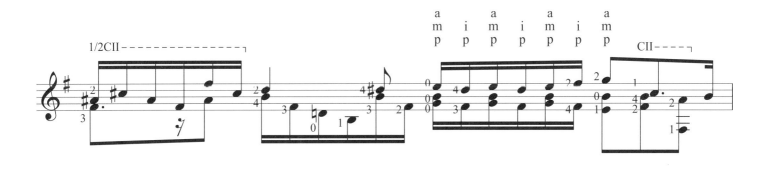

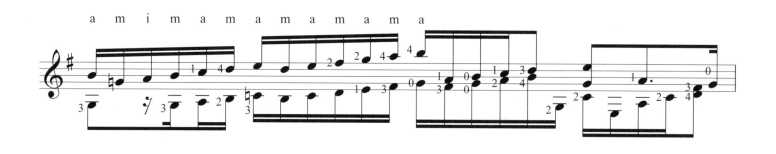

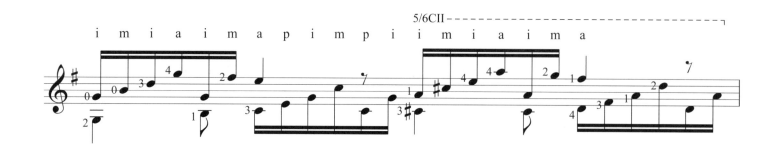

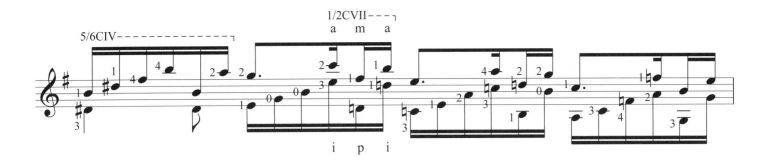
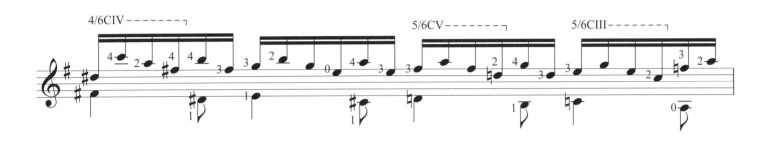
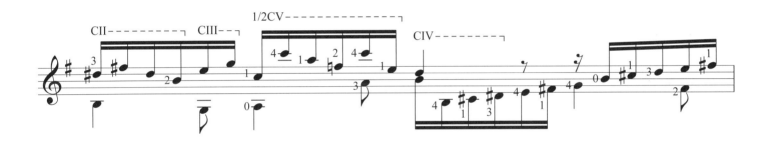

Lady Hundson's Puffe

John Dowland
(1563 - 1626)

Tuning:
(low to high) D-A-D-G-B-E

(♩ = 69)

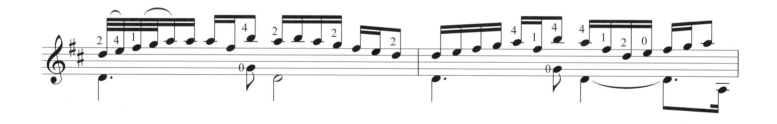

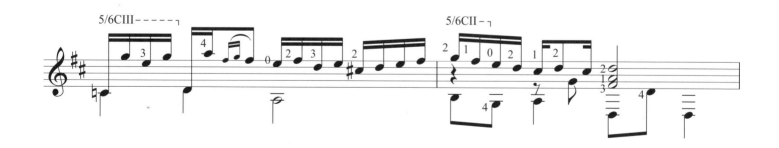

Lágrima

Francisco Tárrega
(1852 - 1909)

Malagueña

Francisco Tárrega
(1852 - 1909)

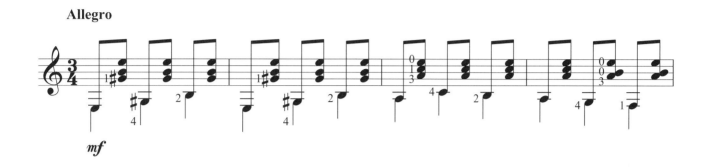

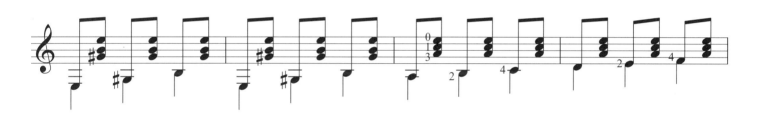

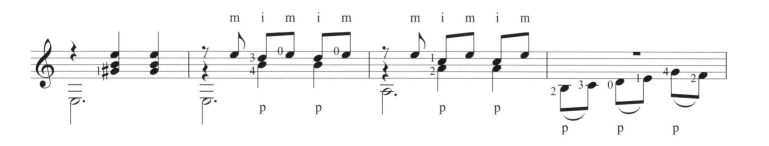

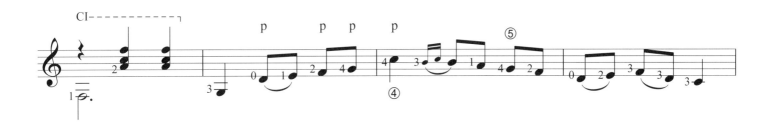

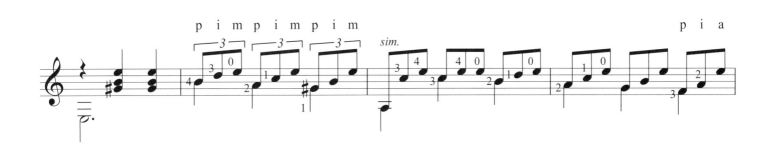

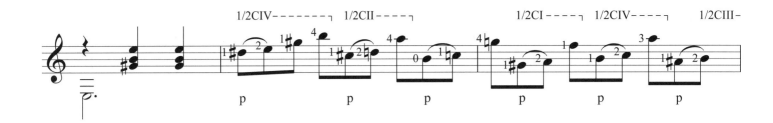

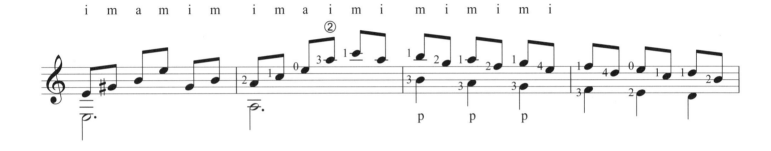

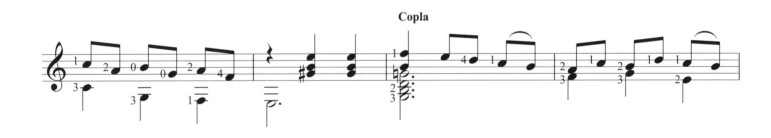

Menuett

Ludovico Roncalli
(1654 - 1713)

Menuetto and Trio
Op. 25

Fernando Sor
(1778 - 1839)

Moderato

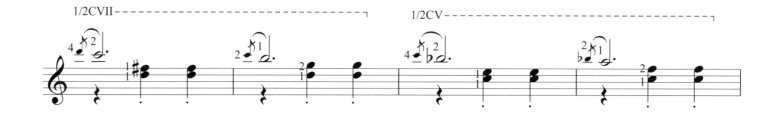

Trio

2nd time, D.C. al Fine

65

Nocturne

Johann Kaspar Mertz
(1806 - 1856)

O Mio Babbino Caro

from GIANNI SCHICCHI

Giacomo Puccini
(1858 - 1924)
Arranged by
John Hill

Andante espressivo

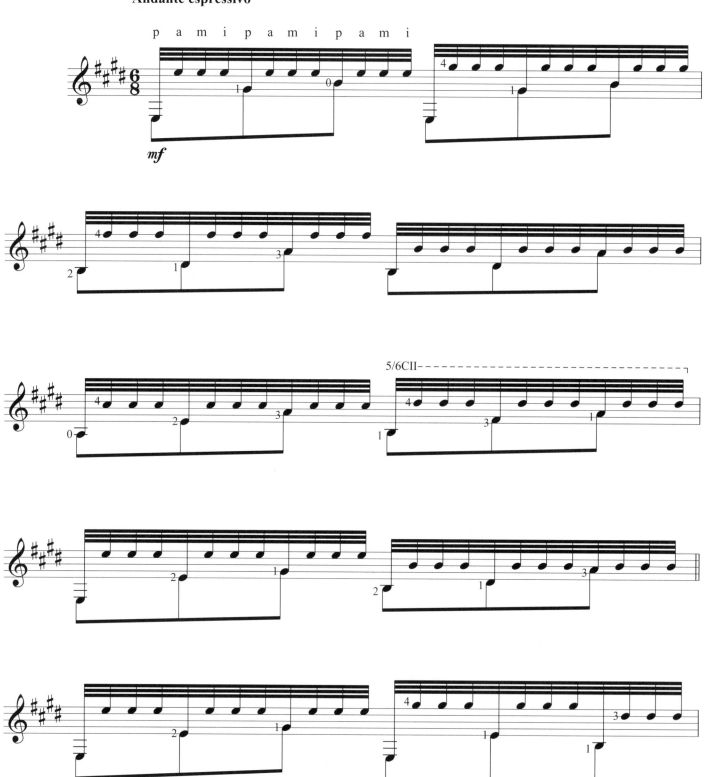

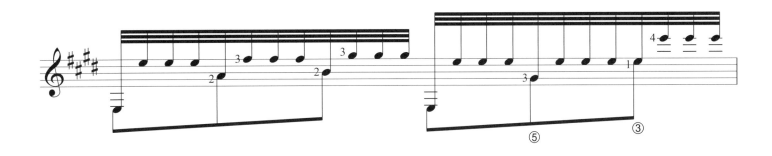

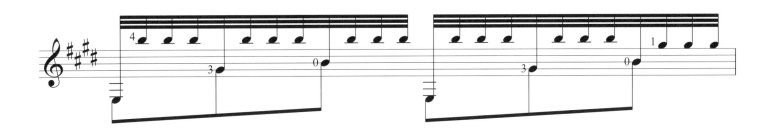

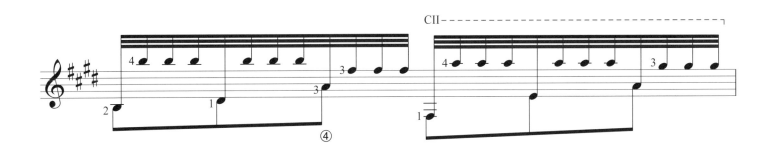

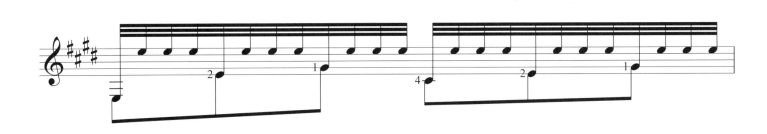

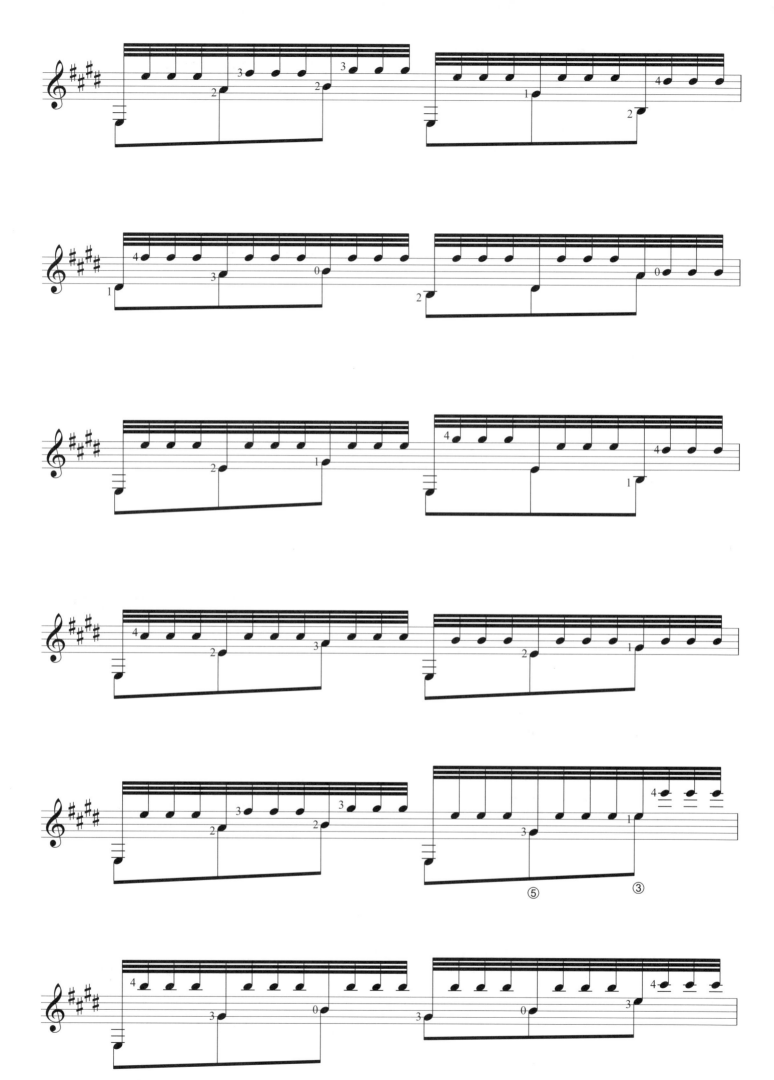

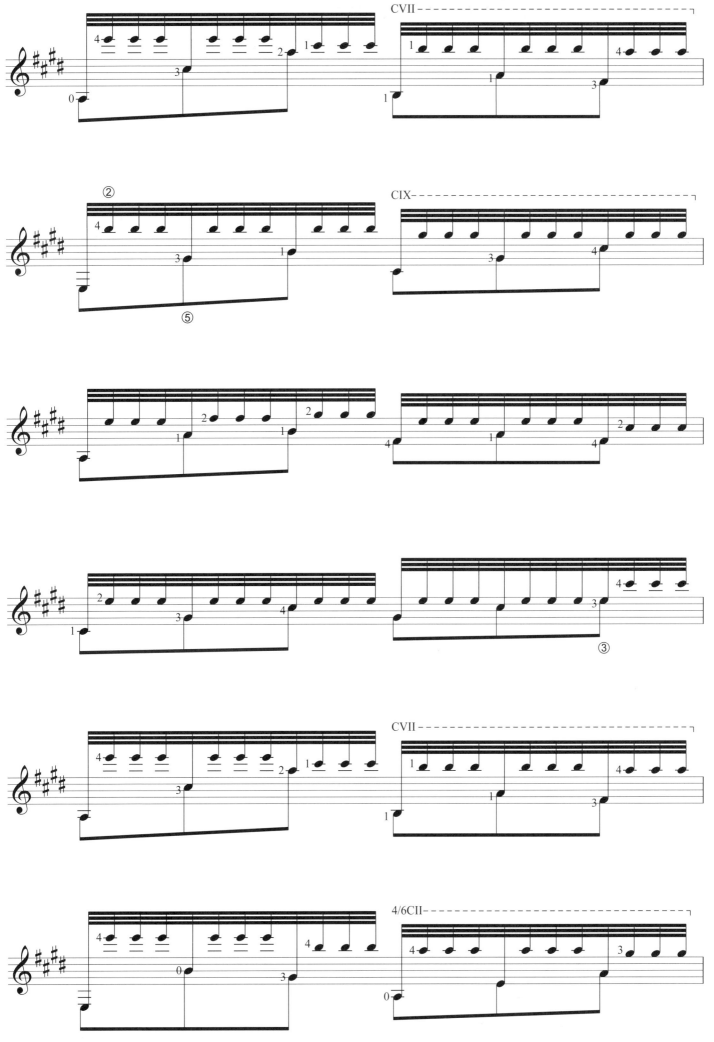

71

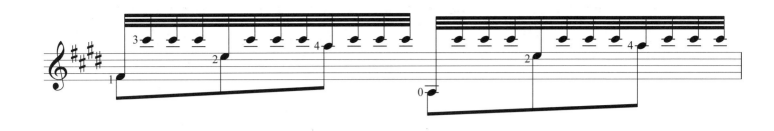

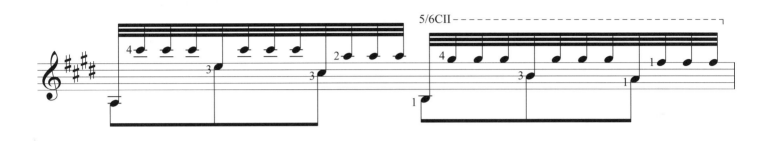

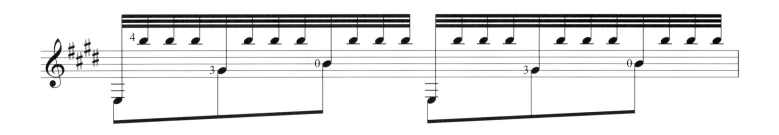

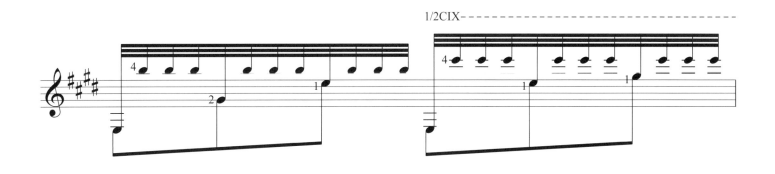

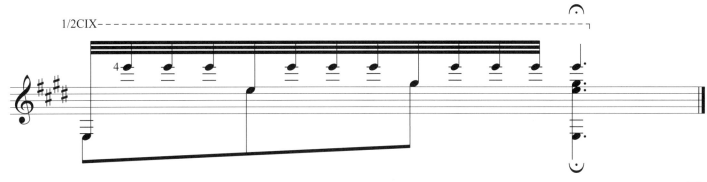

Pavane No. 1

Luis Milan
(c. 1500 - c. 1561)

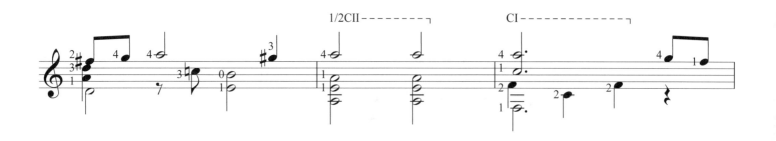

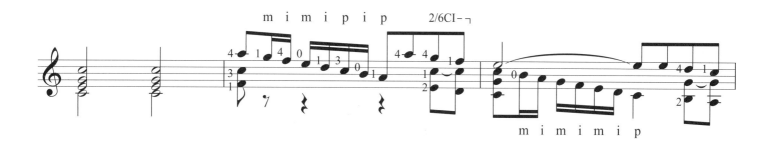

Prelude

Johann Sebastian Bach
(1685 - 1750)

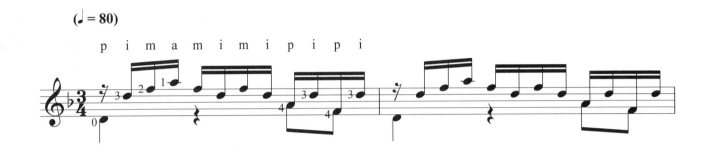

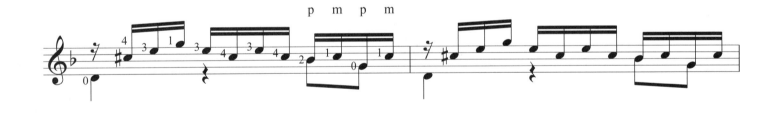

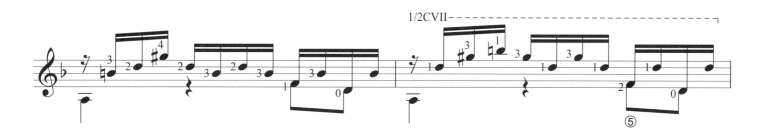

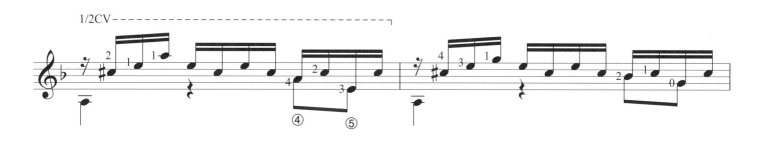

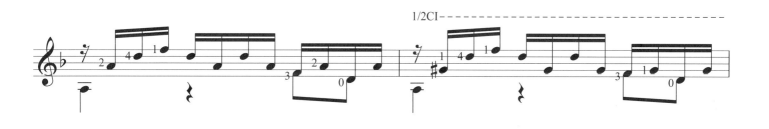

Prelude
BWV 998

Johann Sebastian Bach
(1685 - 1750)

Tuning:
(low to high) D-A-D-G-B-E

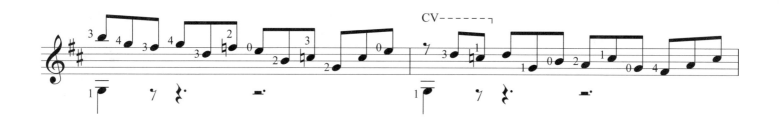

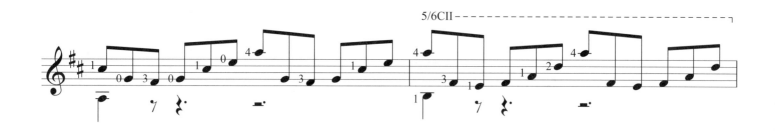
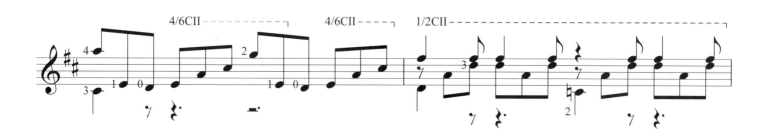

Prelude
from CELLO SUITE NO. 1, BWV 1007

Johann Sebastian Bach
(1685 - 1750)

Tuning:
(low to high) D-A-D-G-B-E

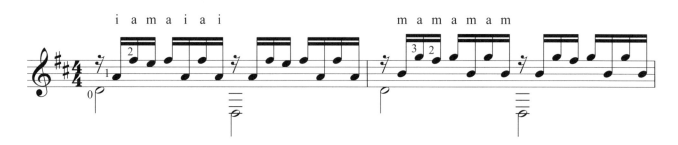

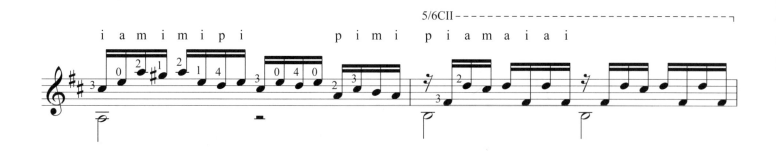

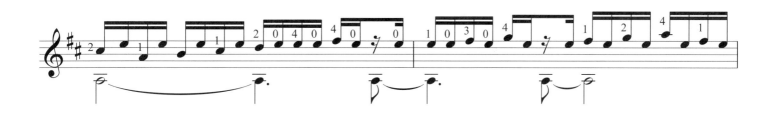

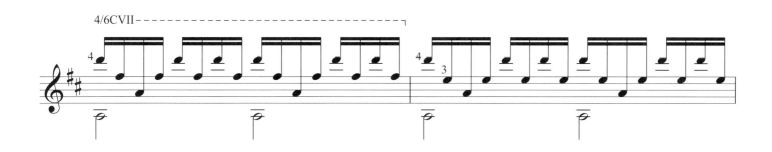

Preludio

Anonymous
(c. 1600)

Tuning:
(low to high) D-A-D-G-B-E

($\quad$ = 84)

Rondo
Op. 22

Fernando Sor
(1778 - 1839)

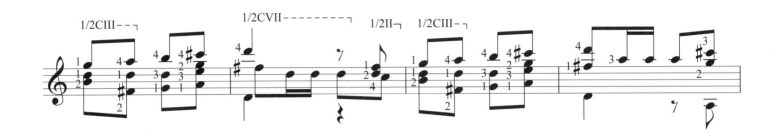

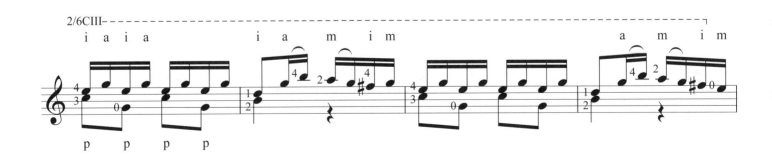

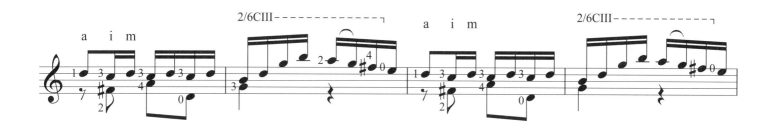

Recuerdos de la Alhambra

Francisco Tárrega
(1852 - 1909)

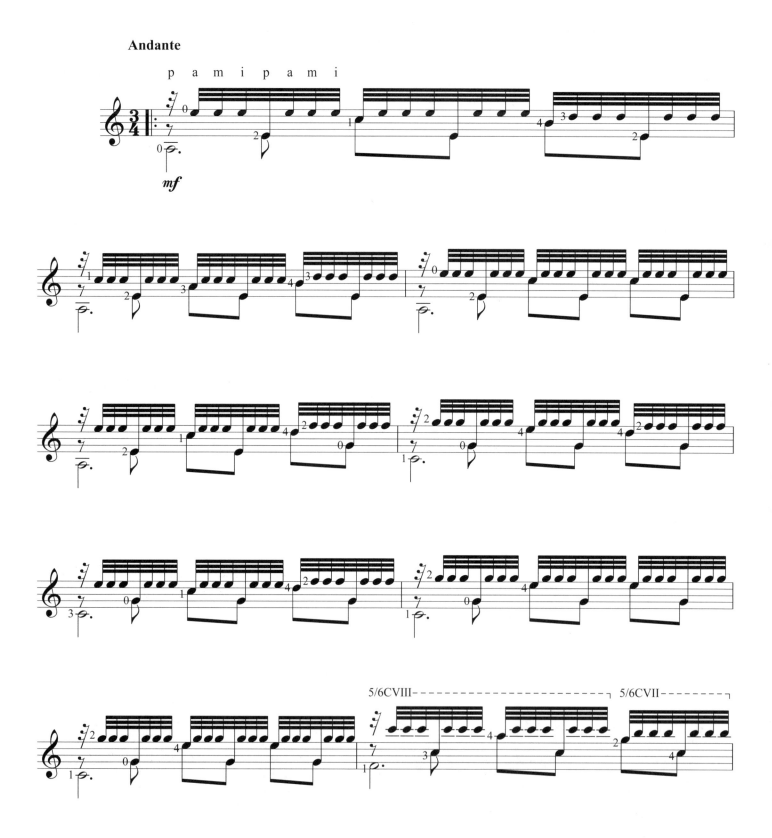

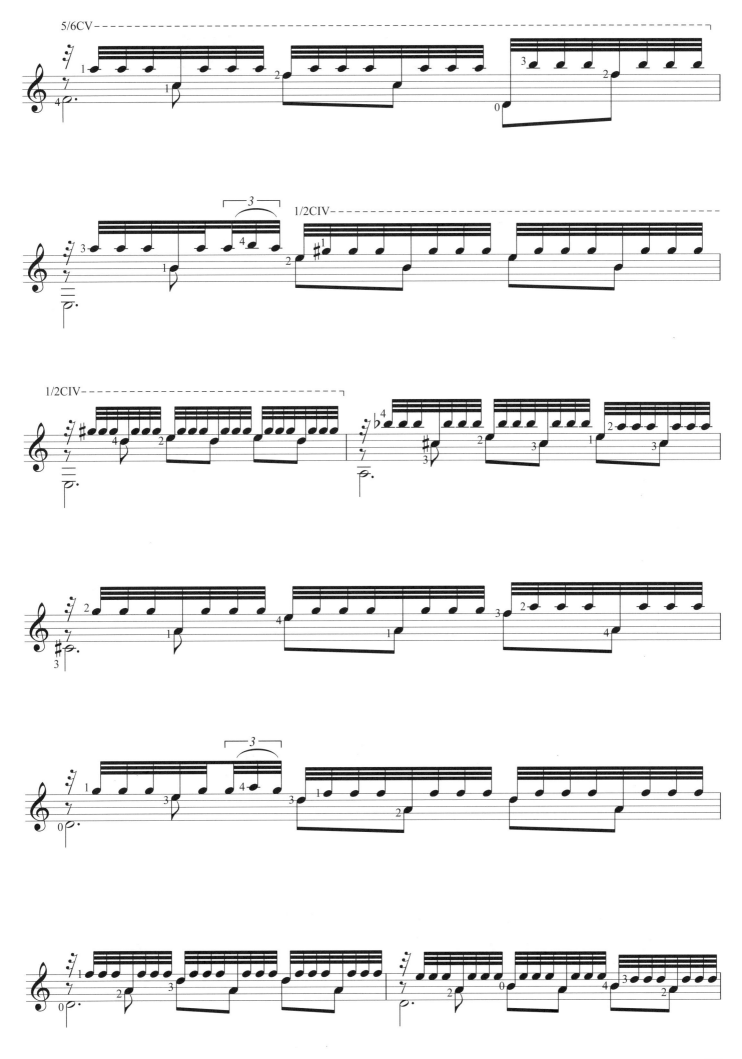

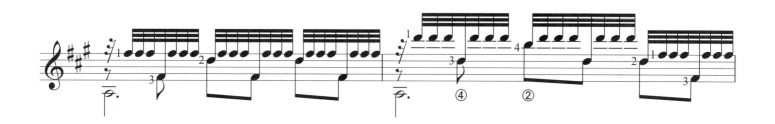

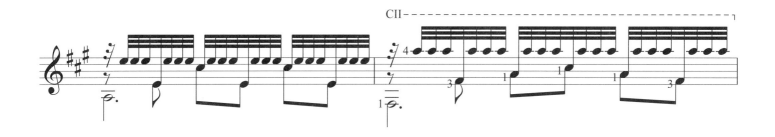

To Coda ⊕

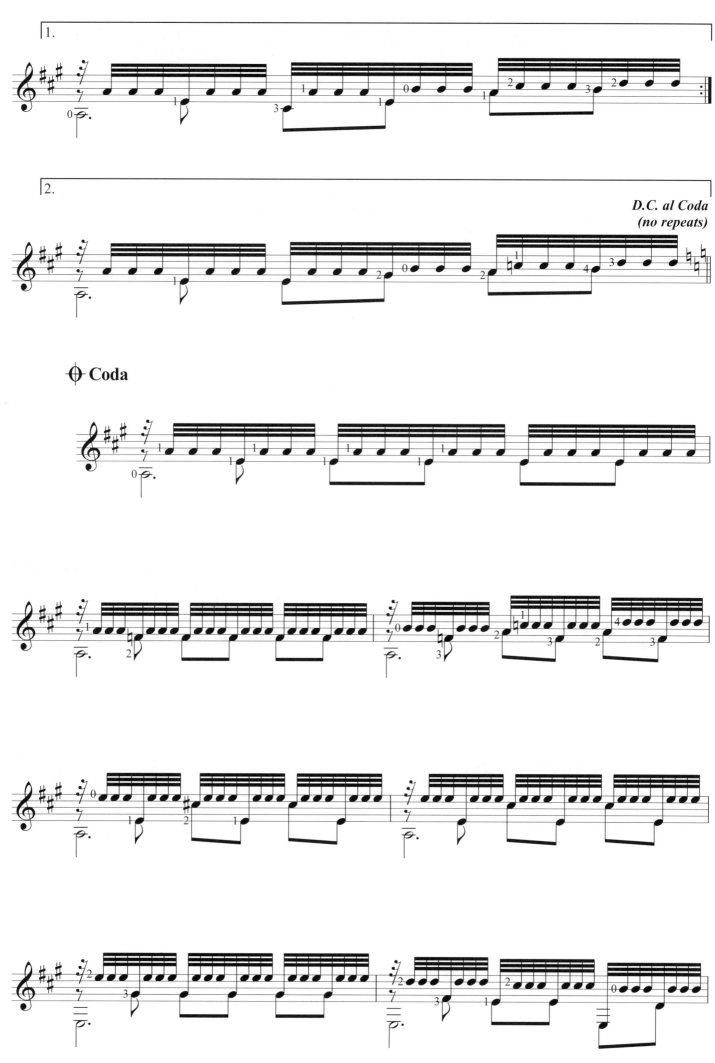

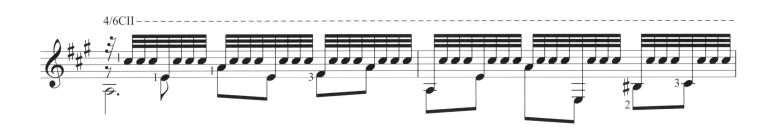

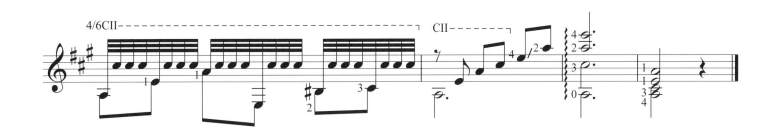

Romanza

Spanish Song

Sarabande

Robert de Visée
(c. 1655 - 1720)

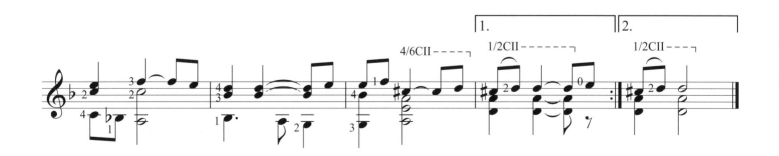

Sonata
K. 32

Domenico Scarlatti
(1685 - 1757)

Sonata
K. 208

Domenico Scarlatti
(1685 - 1757)

108

Study

Op. 60, No. 7

Matteo Carcassi
(1792 - 1853)

Study

Op. 6, No. 6

Fernando Sor
(1778 - 1839)

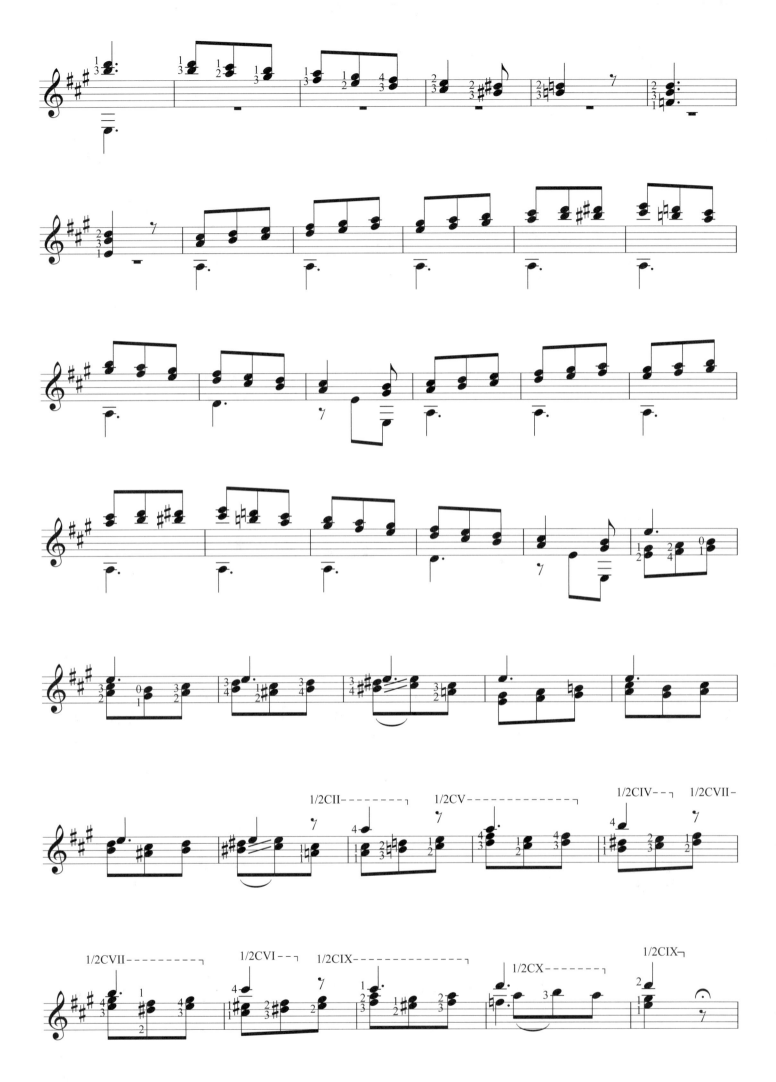

Study
Op. 31, No. 20

Fernando Sor
(1778 - 1839)

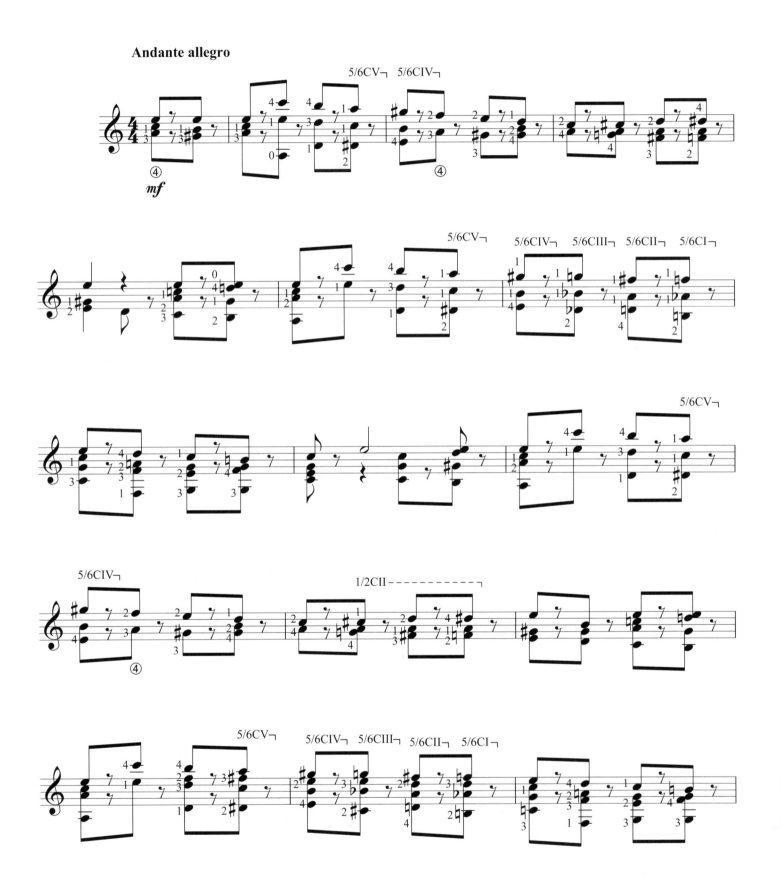

Study

Op. 35, No. 13

Fernando Sor
(1778 - 1839)

Andante

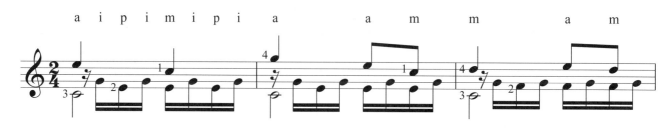

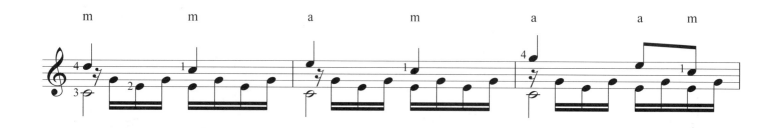

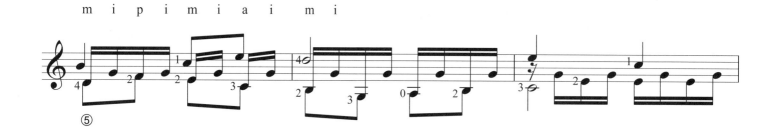

Study
Op. 35, No. 22

Fernando Sor
(1778 - 1839)

Study
Op. 60. No. 3

Matteo Carcassi
(1792 - 1853)

123

Study in E Minor

Dionisio Aguado
(1784 - 1849)

125

Study in E Minor

Francisco Tárrega
(1852 - 1909)

*Optional
harmonics
12th fret

Study in G Major

Dionisio Aguado
(1784 - 1849)

Moderato

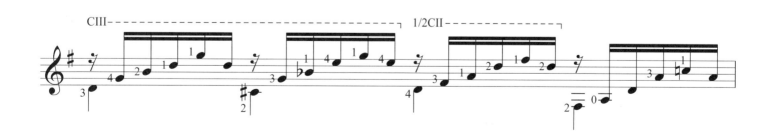

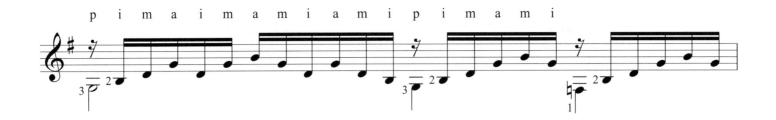

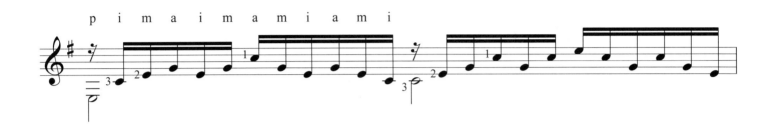

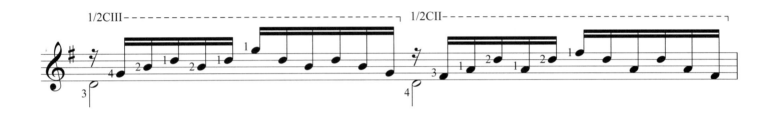

128

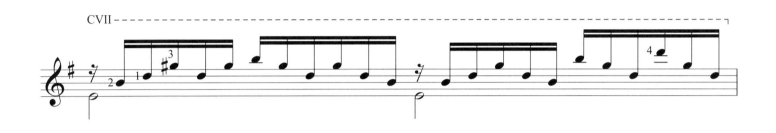

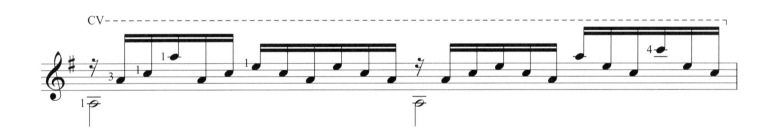

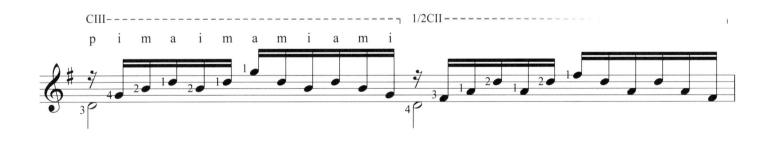

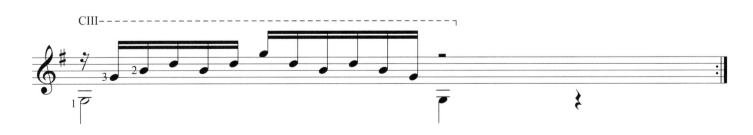

Vivace
from NOCTURNE NO. 3

Johann Kaspar Mertz
(1806 - 1856)

Volte

John Baptiste Besard
(c. 1567 - c. 1625)

Tuning:
(low to high) D-A-D-G-B-E

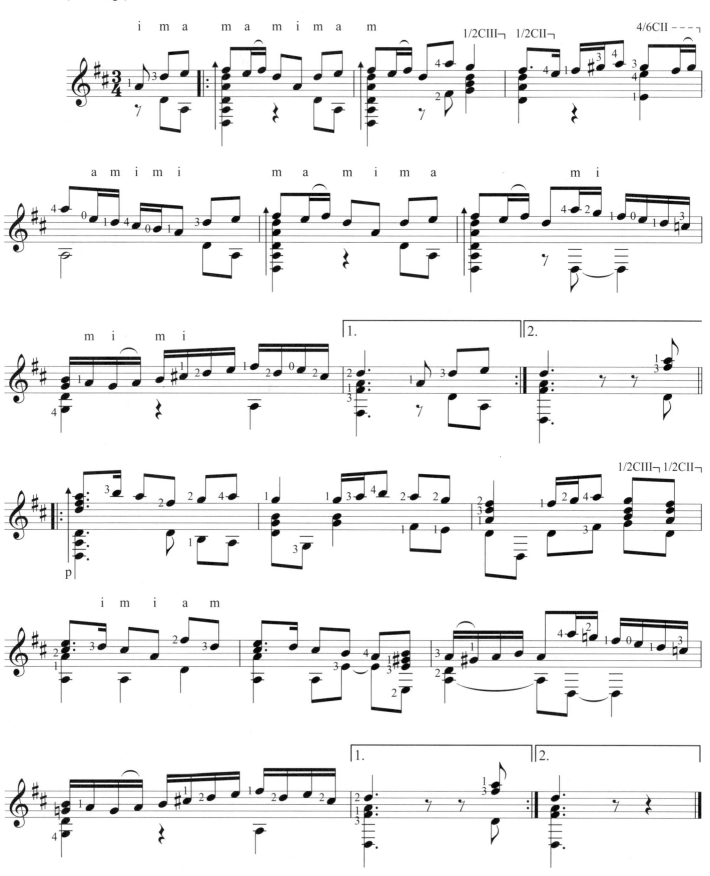

CLASSICAL GUITAR
PUBLICATIONS FROM HAL LEONARD

THE BEATLES FOR CLASSICAL GUITAR

Includes 20 solos from big Beatles hits arranged for classical guitar, complete with left-hand and right-hand fingering. Songs include: All My Loving • And I Love Her • Can't Buy Me Love • Fool on the Hill • From a Window • Hey Jude • If I Fell • Let It Be • Michelle • Norwegian Wood • Obla Di • Ticket to Ride • Yesterday • and more. Features arrangements and an introduction by Joe Washington, as well as his helpful hints on classical technique and detailed notes on how to play each song. The book also covers parts and specifications of the classical guitar, tuning, and Joe's "Strata System" – an easy-reading system applied to chord diagrams.

_____ 00699237 Classical Guitar $19.99

CZERNY FOR GUITAR
INCLUDES TAB
12 SCALE STUDIES FOR CLASSICAL GUITAR
by David Patterson

Adapted from Carl Czerny's *School of Velocity, Op. 299* for piano, this lesson book explores 12 keys with 12 different approaches or "treatments." You will explore a variety of articulations, ranges and technical perspectives as you learn each key. These arrangements will not only improve your ability to play scales fluently, but will also develop your ears, knowledge of the fingerboard, reading abilities, strength and endurance. In standard notation and tablature.

_____ 00701248 .... $9.99

MATTEO CARCASSI – 25 MELODIC AND PROGRESSIVE STUDIES, OP. 60

arr. Paul Henry

One of Carcassi's (1792-1853) most famous collections of classical guitar music – indispensable for the modern guitarist's musical and technical development. Performed by Paul Henry. 49-minute audio accompaniment.

_____ 00696506 Book/CD Pack $17.95

CLASSICAL & FINGERSTYLE GUITAR TECHNIQUES
INCLUDES TAB
by David Oakes • Musicians Institute

This Master Class with MI instructor David Oakes is aimed at any electric or acoustic guitarist who wants a quick, thorough grounding in the essentials of classical and fingerstyle technique. Topics covered include: arpeggios and scales, free stroke and rest stroke, P-i scale technique, three-to-a-string patterns, natural and artificial harmonics, tremolo and rasgueado, and more. The book includes 12 intensive lessons for right and left hand in standard notation & tab, and the CD features 92 solo acoustic tracks.

_____ 00695171 Book/CD Pack $17.99

CLASSICAL GUITAR CHRISTMAS COLLECTION
INCLUDES TAB

Includes classical guitar arrangements in standard notation and tablature for more than two dozen beloved carols: Angels We Have Heard on High • Auld Lang Syne • Ave Maria • Away in a Manger • Canon in D • The First Noel • God Rest Ye Merry, Gentlemen • Hark! the Herald Angels Sing • I Saw Three Ships • Jesu, Joy of Man's Desiring • Joy to the World • O Christmas Tree • O Holy Night • Silent Night • What Child Is This? • and more.

_____ 00699493 Guitar Solo $9.95

CLASSICAL GUITAR WEDDING
INCLUDES TAB

Perfect for players hired to perform for someone's big day, this songbook features 16 classsical wedding favorites arranged for solo guitar in standard notation and tablature. Includes: Air on the G String • Ave Maria • Bridal Chorus • Canon in D • Jesu, Joy of Man's Desiring • Minuet • Sheep May Safely Graze • Wedding March • and more.

_____ 00699563 Solo Guitar with Tab $10.95

CLASSICAL MASTERPIECES FOR GUITAR
INCLUDES TAB

27 works by Bach, Beethoven, Handel, Mendelssohn, Mozart and more transcribed with standard notation and tablature. Now anyone can enjoy classical material regardless of their guitar background. Also features stay-open binding.

_____ 00699312 .... $12.95

MASTERWORKS FOR GUITAR
INCLUDES TAB
Over 60 Favorites from Four Centuries
World's Great Classical Music

Dozens of classical masterpieces: Allemande • Bourree • Canon in D • Jesu, Joy of Man's Desiring • Lagrima • Malaguena • Mazurka • Piano Sonata No. 14 in C# Minor (Moonlight) Op. 27 No. 2 First Movement Theme • Ode to Joy • Prelude No. I (Well-Tempered Clavier).

_____ 00699503 .... $16.95

A MODERN APPROACH TO CLASSICAL GUITAR

by Charles Duncan

This multi-volume method was developed to allow students to study the art of classical guitar within a new, more contemporary framework. For private, class or self-instruction. Book One incorporates chord frames and symbols, as well as a recording to assist in tuning and to provide accompaniments for at-home practice. Book One also introduces beginning fingerboard technique and music theory. Book Two and Three build upon the techniques learned in Book One.

_____ 00695114 Book 1 – Book Only $6.99
_____ 00695113 Book 1 – Book/CD Pack $10.99
_____ 00695116 Book 2 – Book Only $6.99
_____ 00695115 Book 2 – Book/CD Pack $10.99
_____ 00699202 Book 3 – Book Only $7.95
_____ 00695117 Book 3 – Book/CD Pack $10.95
_____ 00695119 Composite Book/CD Pack $29.99

ANDRES SEGOVIA – 20 STUDIES FOR GUITAR

Sor/Segovia

20 studies for the classical guitar written by Beethoven's contemporary, Fernando Sor, revised, edited and fingered by the great classical guitarist Andres Segovia. These essential repertoire pieces continue to be used by teachers and students to build solid classical technique. Features a 50-minute demonstration CD.

_____ 00695012 Book/CD Pack $19.99
_____ 00006363 Book Only $7.99

THE FRANCISCO COLLECTION TÁRREGA
INCLUDES TAB
edited and performed by Paul Henry

Considered the father of modern classical guitar, Francisco Tárrega revolutionized guitar technique and composed a wealth of music that will be a cornerstone of classical guitar repertoire for centuries to come. This unique book/CD pack features 14 of his most outstanding pieces in standard notation and tab, edited and performed on CD by virtuoso Paul Henry. Includes: Adelita • Capricho Árabe • Estudio Brillante • Grand Jota • Lágrima • Malagueña • María • Recuerdos de la Alhambra • Tango • and more, plus bios of Tárrega and Henry.

_____ 00698993 Book/CD Pack $19.99

HAL•LEONARD® CORPORATION
7777 W. BLUEMOUND RD. P.O. BOX 13819 MILWAUKEE, WI 53213

Visit Hal Leonard Online at **www.halleonard.com**